Node for Front-End Developers

Garann Means

Beijing · Cambridge · Farnham · Köln · Sebastopol · Tokyo

Node for Front-End Developers

by Garann Means

Copyright © 2012 Garann Means. All rights reserved.
Printed in the United States of America.

Published by O'Reilly Media, Inc., 1005 Gravenstein Highway North, Sebastopol, CA 95472.

O'Reilly books may be purchased for educational, business, or sales promotional use. Online editions are also available for most titles (*http://my.safaribooksonline.com*). For more information, contact our corporate/institutional sales department: (800) 998-9938 or *corporate@oreilly.com*.

Editor: Simon St. Laurent		**Cover Designer:** Karen Montgomery	
Production Editor: Kristen Borg		**Interior Designer:** David Futato	
Proofreader: O'Reilly Production Services		**Illustrator:** Robert Romano	

Revision History for the First Edition:

2012-01-25   First release

See *http://oreilly.com/catalog/errata.csp?isbn=9781449318833* for release details.

ISBN: 978-1-449-31883-3

[LSI]

1327419600

Table of Contents

Preface v

1. **Getting Node Set Up** 1
   Node and NPM   1
   REPL   2
   File Organization   3

2. **Serving Simple Content** 5
   Writing a Response Manually   5
   Serving a Static Page   6
   Serving Client-Side Assets   8
   Adding In Middleware   10

3. **Interaction with the Client** 13
   Receiving Data from the Querystring   13
   Routing and Receiving Data from a Path   14
   Receiving Data from a POST   15
   Responding to Asynchronous Requests   16
   Real-Time Communication   17

4. **Server-Side Templates** 21
   Creating a Dynamic Page   21
   Partial Templates   24
   Parsing Other File Types   26
   Creating Files on the Fly   27

5. **Data Sources and Flow Control** 29
   Connecting to a Database   29
   Storing Data in Files   32
   Callbacks and Messaging   33

6. Model-View-Controller and Sharing Code 37

    Implementing the MVC Pattern   37

    Out-of-the-Box MVC   42

    Sharing Modules Between the Client and Server   43

Postscript 45

Preface

Node.js has brought the JavaScript revolution of the past few years to the server. JavaScript, it turns out, has uses beyond the client, and many techniques for effective client-side development are applicable on the server side as well. Front-end developers can use their existing skills to work with Node today.

Depending on who you ask, there are several different definitions of "front-end developer". Some of us deal only with client-side languages, relying on other developers to provide data and infrastructure on the server. Others create the server-side tools we need to make the front-end function, things like templates or REST interfaces. What we have in common is that we all probably understand JavaScript, and we are all probably the people responsible for implementing it on the sites we work on.

Even if you never touch server-side development in your work, Node.js is something worth your attention as a front-end developer. The arguments for using Node are well-documented, and you're likely to hear them in the same breath you first hear it mentioned: it's fast, it's scalable, it's evented, it's already got an enthusiastic community of developers building tools. However, if you're already used to coding in JavaScript, the most important reason to consider Node for new sites is a more subjective one: it simply gets out of your way and lets you work.

If you don't often touch server-side development, the process of setting up an application from scratch, organizing files, setting permissions, and doing all the other configuration necessary before you start actually coding might be a bit intimidating. The nice thing about configuration, of course, is that it isn't very hard. It just requires you to remember all of the steps, and in which order to execute them to be successful. As someone who codes websites—not someone who administers web servers—the setup bit might be kind of a painful exercise. This is the great thing about Node. You can do a lot of setup by just writing JavaScript. Adding functionality can be as easy as importing a module. Your paths, your permissions, your session tracking and data persistence are all configured by just writing JavaScript. There are no obscure menus to track down or fragile sets of instructions. You just begin writing code.

A more subtle benefit to Node, when considered from the perspective of those who work on the client-side for a living, is that it operates the same way a client-side application would. Atomic events drive the application, not long sets of instructions. It reacts to its user, rather than publishing static and unchanging information on its own schedule. Node feels more suited to the web than to the desktop, which sets it apart from other popular servers. It feels almost too light to stand alone, like a simple command-line tool instead of the basis for a web framework—and yet it does.

One of the most interesting differences in working with Node is that you can't simply dump a bunch of files into a directory structure and make that public. Files have to be chosen explicitly or in more abstract ways for delivery to the client, and handled by your server-side JavaScript as what they are—content, templates, assets, etc. This can feel tedious when compared to most other servers, which provide the ability to serve static content automatically, but it's easily handled on a larger scale and makes more sense for the type of single-page, client-based application that's becoming prevalent. More and more people who'd consider themselves JavaScript developers are writing applications this way.

 Single-page applications communicate with the server via Ajax, so the user can remain on the same page while still saving their input and receiving updates.

Even without the abstractions and tools that have made Node so popular so quickly, creating a simple application is not difficult and should feel natural to anyone comfortable working with large JavaScript implementations. The basics of how Node serves content and performs essential server tasks are easy to pick up, and will make the popular abstractions you'd be more likely to use in a production application easier to understand.

There are more than 6,000 Node.js modules available in npm as of this writing. You could easily write an entire book covering just the most stable, but this is not that book. Once you begin building serious applications with Node, you will rely heavily on modules. This guide aims to show you how to write applications without them, to provide a better understanding of what Node does by itself, but keep in mind as you're reading that for every problem we'll discuss, there are a multitude of established solutions that are actively maintained, tested, and upgraded. The code samples in this book will show you the theory, but in practice you should take advantage of the excellent work already done by your fellow developers.

Conventions Used in This Book

The following typographical conventions are used in this book:

Constant width
> Used for program listings, as well as within paragraphs to refer to program elements such as variable or function names, databases, data types, environment variables, statements, and keywords.

Constant width italic
> Shows text that should be replaced with user-supplied values or by values determined by context.

Using Code Examples

This book is here to help you get your job done. In general, you may use the code in this book in your programs and documentation. You do not need to contact us for permission unless you're reproducing a significant portion of the code. For example, writing a program that uses several chunks of code from this book does not require permission. Selling or distributing a CD-ROM of examples from O'Reilly books does require permission. Answering a question by citing this book and quoting example code does not require permission. Incorporating a significant amount of example code from this book into your product's documentation does require permission.

We appreciate, but do not require, attribution. An attribution usually includes the title, author, publisher, and ISBN. For example: *"Node for Front-End Developers* by Garann Means (O'Reilly). Copyright 2012 Garann Means, 978-1-449-31883-3."

If you feel your use of code examples falls outside fair use or the permission given above, feel free to contact us at *permissions@oreilly.com*.

Safari® Books Online

Safari Books Online is an on-demand digital library that lets you easily search over 7,500 technology and creative reference books and videos to find the answers you need quickly.

With a subscription, you can read any page and watch any video from our library online. Read books on your cell phone and mobile devices. Access new titles before they are available for print, and get exclusive access to manuscripts in development and post feedback for the authors. Copy and paste code samples, organize your favorites, download chapters, bookmark key sections, create notes, print out pages, and benefit from tons of other time-saving features.

O'Reilly Media has uploaded this book to the Safari Books Online service. To have full digital access to this book and others on similar topics from O'Reilly and other publishers, sign up for free at *http://my.safaribooksonline.com*.

How to Contact Us

Please address comments and questions concerning this book to the publisher:

O'Reilly Media, Inc.
1005 Gravenstein Highway North
Sebastopol, CA 95472
800-998-9938 (in the United States or Canada)
707-829-0515 (international or local)
707-829-0104 (fax)

We have a web page for this book, where we list errata, examples, and any additional information. You can access this page at:

http://shop.oreilly.com/product/0636920023258.do

To comment or ask technical questions about this book, send email to:

bookquestions@oreilly.com

For more information about our books, courses, conferences, and news, see our website at *http://www.oreilly.com*.

Find us on Facebook: *http://facebook.com/oreilly*

Follow us on Twitter: *http://twitter.com/oreillymedia*

Watch us on YouTube: *http://www.youtube.com/oreillymedia*

CHAPTER 1

Getting Node Set Up

Depending on your environment, Node is easy to set up or *very* easy to set up. Node runs on Unix-compatible systems and, more recently, Windows. The former means it runs on Macs, Linux machines, and most environments you're likely to be developing for. There are companies offering Node hosting with all kinds of great features like monitoring tools and deployment via version control tools like Git. However, you can also install Node on any server you can SSH into where you have the ability to create files and directories.

For purposes of getting something running, let's assume you're installing Node locally on a Mac. We'll highlight the differences for Windows and remote server setup as we go.

Node and NPM

There are numerous ways to install Node itself, depending on your environment. The easiest option is to download one of the installers available for Windows or Mac from the Node website (these include npm, as well). You can also install it in one line using Homebrew or the Advance Packaging Tool. On any supported operating system, if you have Git installed, you can clone Node directly from the repository and build it yourself.

Since it's fairly universal, let's look at getting Node from GitHub. This assumes that Git is already installed and available.

```
$ git clone git://github.com/joyent/node.git
$ cd node
$ git checkout v0.6.6
$ ./configure
$ make
$ make install
```

All we're doing is cloning the GitHub repository, running a configuration script, and then building and installing Node. Pay special attention to the third line, though, because we're also switching to the branch containing the most recent stable version of Node. That changes frequently, so if you decide to install from the command line, check the Node.js website first to find out what the current stable version is, or use `git tag` to list available versions.

It's no longer necessary to install npm separately, but if you need or want to for some reason, command-line installation is very straightforward. For all environments where npm is currently supported, the preferred method of installation is Curl:

```
$ curl http://npmjs.org/install.sh | sh
```

 npm is Node's package manager. It maintains a registry of Node modules and allows one-line installation and version management of third-party packages. You can find modules in npm from the command line using `npm search` *search term*.

REPL

REPL stands for Read-Eval-Print-Loop, and is a utility included with Node that can be very handy when you're getting started. It works like the debug console in your browser and you can execute whatever commands you want. You don't need to do anything to install it—you'll have it available from the command line wherever Node is available. Before even creating an application you can start poking around and see what Node can do by typing `node` on the command line. If you don't specify an application to run, you get the REPL instead.

After typing `node` at the command prompt, you can test a few simple lines of JavaScript, and they should evaluate as normal:

```
> ["Hello","World"].join(" ")
'Hello World'
> 2 + 3
5
```

You can exit the REPL by pressing Ctrl+C.

Let's say you're researching modules to manage asynchronous code paths in your project. There are numerous modules to handle asynchronous code and flow control —let's assume you've found a couple you'd like to compare, but neither has a documented API (in reality, the one we're using below has very nice documentation). To get a better picture of what's included, you can install them with npm and then use the REPL to investigate them. If you installed the `async` module, for instance, you could do this:

```
$ node
> var async = require("async");
undefined
> console.dir(async);
```

That will cause the module to spit out a list of its properties, which you can investigate further from that point, should you so desire. Of course you could just read the source, but it's useful to know you can open the REPL and see exactly what Node sees. You can also use Tab to auto-complete function and variable names within your code, which may be a faster reference than searching online if you're in the midst of testing something.

File Organization

With Node installed, we can begin creating the scaffolding for a web application. Since we control how our application serves files, we can put them almost anywhere we want. There are, however, a few conventions it makes sense for us to follow. It's expected that the main application file we want to run is in the root directory of the site, as is the `package.json` file (which we'll create below). Some common directories we might expect to find in the root would include:

node_modules
>   Your locally installed modules from npm

lib
>   Utilities and other custom modules that belong to your application

public, www, or similar
>   The static, client-side piece of your application

When setting up a directory structure, all that really matters is whether it makes sense to you. If you'll be using the Model-View-Controller (MVC) pattern for your application, you may choose to have `models`, `views`, and `controllers` directories in your root. If you're going to use the Express application framework or model your application's organization on Express, you may have a root directory called `routes`. Aside from keeping your organization clear and consistent in case someone else needs to work with it, being in control of how your application finds and delivers files means you can put them wherever you think they belong.

We also want to create a `package.json` file, which is a manifest for our application. This file is especially important for modules that will be published or shared, but it should also be present for our local application. There are lots of things we might add to a `package.json` file, but for now let's create a simple one with some meta information about the application and a couple of dependencies:

```json
{
  "name": "myNodeApp",
  "author": "Jaime Developer",
  "description": "my test node.js application",
  "version": "0.0.1",
  "dependencies": {
    "connect": "1.8.x",
    "express": "2.5.x"
  },
  "engine": "0.6.x",
  "main": "app.js"
}
```

Most of those keys are exactly what they sound like. The last two, engine and main, refer to the version of Node and the path to the main application file, respectively. The dependencies object is important to note, as it will come in handy if we ever want to move this application. If that object contains all the npm modules our application uses and their correct versions, we can run the command npm install from the root of our application's new home to install all the required modules at once.

CHAPTER 2

Serving Simple Content

Because serving content is a web server's reason for being, there are thousands of Node modules available to automate the various ways of doing so, or to wrap that entire set of functions up in a robust framework. Working with what Node includes natively, however, provides a beneficial illustration of how it works as a web server, and creating simple applications with its out-of-the-box utilities is fairly trivial.

Writing a Response Manually

The first thing we'll do in any web application we write in Node is to require a module allowing us to actually serve a website. Most common server tasks are part of the http or https modules. At minimum, any web application will need to import one of these (or another module which has one or the other as a dependency) using the require function. Node's built-in dependency management is similar to CommonJS, and require masks the complexity of searching for the desired module and avoiding redundancy.

```
var http = require("http");
```

Once the http module is available, we can create a server and ask it to begin listening for requests. The createServer() function has only one parameter: the callback that will execute whenever a request is received. The listen() function that starts the server can take several arguments, but for a simple server we just need to provide the port and, optionally, the host IP:

```
var http = require("http");

http.createServer(function(req, res) {
  var html = "<!doctype html>" +
      "<html><head><title>Hello world</title></head>" +
      "<body><h1>Hello, world!</h1></body></html>";

  res.writeHead(200, {
    // set the type of content we're returning
    "Content-Type": "text/html",
```

```
      // set the length of our content
      "Content-Length": html.length
    });
    // end the response, sending it and returning our HTML
    res.end(html);
  }).listen(8000, "127.0.0.1");
```

The callback in createServer() is listening for a request event, a built-in event type defined by the http module. The event handler receives two arguments: the request and a response object. Since we're not doing anything dynamic to begin with, we only need to worry about the response we'll build to send back to the client. The minimum we need to build a response the client can render is the function end(). The end() function will do double duty ending the response and writing content to it, the latter of which can also be done with write(). The writeHead() function creates a header for the file we're sending to the client, indicating what the browser should do with it. We don't actually need it here, since it's mimicking the defaults, but we will later on. The canonical Node Hello World example uses these two functions to spit out a little text, but we can go slightly further and return proper HTML.

If that worked out, we ought to see a very minimal web page when we start our application, which is as simple as typing node *name of file* from the command prompt. Depending on how you've structured your files, you probably have a single container directory per application, in which case you could name the application file app.js or server.js (or anything else, really, but you'll see those two frequently). If you're sharing a directory with other apps or services or just don't like the convention of giving the main application file a generic name, you can call it something more specific to your app. But let's say you called it app.js. You start your application up by returning to the command prompt in your root application directory on your server and typing:

```
$ node app.js
```

By default, the server will listen to localhost, or 127.0.0.1, but we've also explicitly provided the host above. Unless there's an error, the command above won't produce any output in the terminal window, but if you go to 127.0.0.1:8000 or localhost:8000 from a browser at this point, you'll see your Hello World page show up.

Serving a Static Page

Realistically, we won't want to manually write out the contents of each page we want to serve from within our JavaScript. It's much more maintainable to store our HTML as HTML in separate files.

Since our pure HTML page will contain no logic, we can move it to the front-end of our application and create it in our public folder (or whatever the equivalent is in your directory structure). In this example we'll adhere to predictable conventions from other servers and call our main page index.html, but feel free to name yours whatever makes sense. Since we're writing our own server, there's no defined list of filenames it will try to locate to get the default content for the current directory, so if you use those conventions, the only advantage is predictability. Let's start by creating that page and moving the same HTML we were writing in JavaScript into it:

```
<!doctype html>
<html>
  <head>
    <title>Hello world</title>
  </head>
  <body>
    <h1>Hello, world!</h1>
  </body>
</html>
```

To ensure that our HTML page gets served correctly, we'll need to change our server code to investigate the request being made of it. Instead of providing the same response for anything the user requests, we should check whether the requested file's extension is .html, make sure the resource actually exists, and if it does, load and return the body of the corresponding file. To do that, we'll need to rewrite the body of our createServer() callback:

```
var http = require("http"),
  // utilities for working with file paths
  path = require("path"),
  // utilities for accessing the file system
  fs = require("fs");

http.createServer(function(req, res) {

  // look for a filename in the URL, default to index.html
  var filename = path.basename(req.url) || "index.html",
    ext = path.extname(filename),
    // __dirname is a built-in variable containing the path where the code is running
    localPath = __dirname + "/public/";

  if (ext == ".html") {
    localPath += filename;
    // verify that this file actually exists and load it, or else return a 404
    path.exists(localPath, function(exists) {
      if (exists) {
        getFile(localPath, res);
      } else {
        res.writeHead(404);
        res.end();
      }
    });
  }

}).listen(8000);
```

Loading the file to be served is now handled in a separate function, which we can add right after createServer():

```
function getFile(localPath, res) {
  // read the file in and return it, or return a 500 if it can't be read
  fs.readFile(localPath, function(err, contents) {
    if (!err) {
      // use defaults instead of res.writeHead()
      res.end(contents);
    } else {
      res.writeHead(500);
      res.end();
    }
  });
}
```

Suddenly our simple application returning its simple file looks pretty serious. However, all that's really changed from our Hello World is that we've created additional functionality, and additional branching in case something goes wrong with that functionality. We've taken the first step toward abstracting the new functionality out for later reuse by moving the reading of the file into its own function. This also helps avoid a level of nested callbacks, which is a nice bonus in a platform where almost everything is asynchronous and callbacks can stack up very quickly.

If you restart your application at this point, you should see your `index.html` page delivered to the client when you hit your local URL and specify that filename. We've also set `index.html` up as a default, so if you leave the filename off, you should still see `index.html` or whatever fallback you've defined for the `filename` variable. You should also be able to add a second plain HTML page and navigate directly to that without changing the application code.

> Restarting a Node app can be done manually or automated. If the process is still running on your command line, Ctrl+C will end it. You can then use the `node app.js` command to start it up again with your changes. Restarting this way can quickly become annoying, so it may be worth investigating the numerous tools available to do this automatically whenever your code changes.

Serving Client-Side Assets

Serving other client-side assets like CSS, images, and client-side JavaScript (of course) looks very similar to serving HTML. We'll need to add some additional robustness to the code we've already built, but a few changes will allow us to provide resources to the client pretty easily. All we actually need to change is the way we set the `Content-Type` in our response, which means it's necessary to modify the default header. This time, instead of changing the status code we're returning, we'll change that header property. We'll cheat a little bit right now to make this more straightforward and assume that all URLs to resources will be relative to the root of our application.

The first change we'll make is to store any directories in the requested URL, so that if our resources are organized into directories, we'll still be able to use this same function to access them. We'll remove the first character, since that should always be a slash, to make it easier down the line to find out whether or not the file we want is in a subdirectory:

```
var filename = path.basename(req.url) || "index.html",
  ext = path.extname(filename),
  dir = path.dirname(req.url).substring(1),
  localPath = __dirname + "/public/";
```

The next thing we need to change is the section where we're testing the file extension to make sure we can serve it. We could just test for a bunch of different extensions, but it'll be easier to just create a hash of the extensions we want to support and the MIME types they map to. We'll add that below our module imports, so all of our code has access to it:

```
var http = require("http"),
  path = require("path"),
  fs = require("fs"),
  extensions = {
    ".html": "text/html",
    ".css": "text/css",
    ".js": "application/javascript",
    ".png": "image/png",
    ".gif": "image/gif",
    ".jpg": "image/jpeg"
  };
```

Now that we have all our extensions and their MIME types listed out, we can change the code that checks for the existence of the file and calls the getFile() function. We'll want to test for all of our extensions, add the directory to our path if the file is in a subdirectory, and pass the correct MIME type to the getFile() function when we call it:

```
if (extensions[ext]) {
  localPath += (dir ? dir + "/" : "") + filename;
  path.exists(localPath, function(exists) {
    if (exists) {
      getFile(localPath, extensions[ext], res);
    } else {
      res.writeHead(404);
      res.end();
    }
  });
}
```

The last change we'll make is to the signature of the getFile() function and the 200 response path within it, so that we send the correct Content-Type for whatever kind of file we return:

```
function getFile(localPath, mimeType, res) {
  fs.readFile(localPath, function(err, contents) {
    if (!err) {
      res.writeHead(200, {
        "Content-Type": mimeType,
        "Content-Length": contents.length
      });
      res.end(contents);
    } else {
      res.writeHead(500);
      res.end();
    }
  });
}
```

At this point, if you add CSS or JavaScript to your existing page or pages, the application should serve those resources. For right now, their URLs will need to take the form /filename.extension or /directory/filename.extension, but aside from that, you should be able to add and serve resources from anywhere under your public directory.

Adding In Middleware

It's important to understand what Node is doing under the hood when it's serving files, especially since it isn't actually that complicated. All the work we expect Apache, Nginx, and other servers to do for us automatically can be reduced to simple programming, little more than parsing a string. It's also good to know what Node has built-in for those tasks. However, it's safer, more efficient, and far more common to use one or more of the third-party tools already written to do this sort of work.

 In the context of a web server, middleware is a layer between the guts of the server and the code you're writing to run on it that provides a set of abstractions anyone writing code for the platform will be likely to need. It differs from other modules you might pull into your application in that it exists as a buffer between Node and your app, not a utility used within your app.

Connect is an overwhelmingly popular Node middleware framework that provides the basis for other popular solutions like Express. One of the tools Connect provides is the static module, which does exactly what we've done above, but in a more robust fashion. If we add in Connect, we can write the same application with far less code:

```
var connect = require("connect");

connect(connect.static(__dirname + "/public")).listen(8000);
```

The code you see above replaces everything we wrote in the last example in just two lines. To actually run this, you'll need to use npm to install Connect. Installing modules with npm is extremely simple. There are optional flags you can set and other tricks npm can do, but a simple installation from the command line looks almost like how you'd describe what you're doing in English. Though they can be installed globally, modules are installed locally in the `node_modules` directory by default, so make sure to run the command from the root directory of your application:

```
$ npm install connect
```

Once you have Connect installed, you'll find the `static.js` file that provides the logic for `connect.static()` above in `node_modules/connect/middleware` and you can take a look at the source for yourself. What you'll find is a completed version of the work we began earlier, with further handling of edge cases and a less brittle API. Because serving static files can be as simple as agreeing to provide any files within our `public` directory, the only configuration we absolutely must do is setting that path to our front-end files.

Working with client-side JavaScript libraries may have taught you to treat third-party extensions with suspicion, but the two lines of code above are an example of how that's slightly different in Node. Node is your platform, and it's up to you to create the server and the application. While modules that provide additional functionality to an application make a neat analogy to client-side plugins, modules to abstract out common server functions map more readily to Apache modules. Web applications need a lot of the same basic utilities to serve files, so there's nothing wrong with using a well-supported module to provide that functionality. As a matter of fact, it's considered a best practice.

Interaction with the Client

All but the simplest of sites will eventually need to send data to and receive data from the server. It's great that our server is delivering static files—we'll need that for our CSS, images, and other resources—but at some point we'll probably want to be able to serve a single-page application where static requests don't play as large a role. The great thing about Node is that, as JavaScript developers, we can have complete control over our API on both the client and server, and even reuse some of our code on both sides. But let's start with setting up handling for simple GET and POST requests.

Receiving Data from the Querystring

The easiest way to pass data to the server is by adding it to the querystring. This way we don't have to do a lot of client-side setup to test our code, and if we take advantage of any of the popular client-side *or* server-side frameworks, we'll probably send parameters using routes, which is not so terribly different.

Node provides a `querystring` module, so we don't have to do as much parsing of the request URL to get to the querystring data. The one thing we need to do is trim the querystring, since the `querystring` module separates out the pieces, but doesn't separate the querystring from the rest of the URL. After adding the new module, we can reuse the basic Hello World code we wrote, getting it to take and process some input without needing too many changes:

```
var http = require("http"),
  querystring = require("querystring");

http.createServer(function(req, res) {
  // parse everything after the "?" into key/value pairs
  var qs = querystring.parse(req.url.split("?")[1]),
    // property names are the same as in the querystring
    userName = qs.firstName + " " + qs.lastName,
    html = "<!doctype html>" +
      "<html><head><title>Hello " + userName + "</title></head>" +
      "<body><h1>Hello, " + userName + "!</h1></body></html>";
```

```
    res.end(html);
  }).listen(8000);
```

Now, navigating to our application with a URL like `localhost:8000?firstName`
`=Jaime&lastName=Developer` should provide a personalized Hello World page that uses
the name we submitted.

Routing and Receiving Data from a Path

Routing is another thing we can get from middleware, but it's nothing so complicated
that we couldn't implement it ourselves if we had to. Routing will let us extract data
from a URL's path in addition to its querystring. A route usually defines, at minimum,
the method of the request, the pattern the route matches, and a callback function to
be executed when a matching request is received. It's pretty simple to check those
things, although we'd need to add robustness for a real-world application.

Let's say we want our application above, instead of checking for a first and last name
in the querystring, to look for them in the path of the URL. Let's say also that this
functionality lives on its own virtual "page", sayHello, and we'll pass in parameters
like /sayHello/*first name*/*last name*:

```
var http = require("http"),
  url = require("url");

http.createServer(function(req, res) {
  // split out parts of the path
  var path = url.parse(req.url).pathname.split("/");
  // handle GET requests to /sayHello/
  if (req.method == "GET" && path[1] == "sayHello") {
    var userName = path[2] + " " + path[3],
      html = "<!doctype html>" +
        "<html><head><title>Hello " + userName + "</title></head>" +
        "<body><h1>Hello, " + userName + "!</h1></body></html>";

    res.end(html);
  }
}).listen(8000);
```

Of course, that's a somewhat fragile and non-scalable way to deal with routing—for
example, we have to dump the first element in our path array since our path starts with
a slash—so let's look quickly at how it's done with Connect:

```
var connect = require("connect");

connect(
  connect.static(__dirname + "/public"),
  // create a router to handle application paths
  connect.router(function(app) {
    app.get("/sayHello/:firstName/:lastName", function(req, res) {
      var userName = req.params.firstName + " " + req.params.lastName,
        html = "<!doctype html>" +
```

```
                   "<html><head><title>Hello " + userName + "</title></head>" +
                   "<body><h1>Hello, " + userName + "!</h1></body></html>";

            res.end(html);
        });
    })
).listen(8000);
```

It should be possible to find some similarities between what's happening in the first example and what's going on in the second. By convention, most routers convert variables prefixed by a colon to properties of the `req.params` object. Routing goes beyond just handling GET and POST, as well, and will allow you to handle all the proper HTTP methods. With as large a collection of paths and methods as you need, you can create a set of endpoints rich enough for any application.

Receiving Data from a POST

The more traditional model of getting user data—taking a POST request from a form —might not be the first thing you'd think of using Node for, but of course it's still necessary. In fact, handling a POST may provide one of the most concise explanations of how Node differs from other server setups, and how it might make more sense in the context of the way the web actually works. The `ServerRequest` object (the `req` argument in our callbacks) has no property containing the parameters passed along in a POST, but it *is* an EventEmitter. EventEmitter is the generic object type in Node for things that—as you might expect—emit events. Rather than looking at a property on `req` to find posted data, we add an event subscriber to listen for it.

All EventEmitter subscribers, including the subscribers belonging to `ServerRequest`, are created by the `on()` function, which needs an event type and a callback as parameters, at minimum. (The `addListener()` function does the same thing.) The request data will come across in chunks, so we're not waiting to receive all of it before other code can run. Here, we'll create listeners for the receipt of data and the end of the request, saving all the chunks of data, but not expecting it to be present until the request is complete:

```
var http = require("http"),
  fs = require("fs"),
  querystring = require("querystring");

http.createServer(function(req, res) {
  var data = "";

  // serve static form
  if (req.method == "GET") {
    getFile(__dirname + "/public/simpleForm.html", res);
  }

  // handle form post
  if (req.method == "POST") {
    req.on("data", function(chunk) {
```

```
      // append received data
      data += chunk;
    });
    req.on("end", function() {
      // get key/value pairs from received data
      var params = querystring.parse(data),
        userName = params.firstName + " " + params.lastName,
        html = "<!doctype html>" +
          "<html><head><title>Hello " + userName + "</title></head>" +
          "<body><h1>Hello, " + userName + "!</h1></body></html>";

      res.end(html);
    });
  }
}).listen(8000);

function getFile(localPath, res) {
  // ...
}
```

There are a few extra pieces in here to serve a static, hardcoded file (`simpleForm.html`) when the user first accesses the site, assuming we've pulled in the `getFile()` function we used before. If that page had a form containing fields with the names `firstName` and `lastName`, submitting the form to our application ought to produce our test page again.

As before, we can save ourselves a lot of code with the use of middleware from Connect, and as before, this pattern is similar to what you'll see in most frameworks for parsing the body of a posted request. We're using the `bodyParser` module, which automatically adds the posted data to `req.body`. Other than that, the code is much the same as in previous examples:

```
var connect = require("connect");

connect(
  connect.static(__dirname + "/public"),
  connect.bodyParser(),
  function(req, res) {
    var userName = req.body.firstName + " " + req.body.lastName,
      html = "<!doctype html>" +
        "<html><head><title>Hello " + userName + "</title></head>" +
        "<body><h1>Hello, " + userName + "!</h1></body></html>";

    res.end(html);
  }
).listen(8000);
```

Responding to Asynchronous Requests

So far, we've looked at ways of getting data to the server that haven't changed much since most of us first experienced the web. More and more front-end developers these days, however, eschew those methods entirely in favor of the single-page app. Single-page apps, of course, rely on Ajax.

It's useful to begin working with Node without the addition of niceties like frameworks and templating when it comes to handling asynchronous requests. Because we're still pretty close to the metal, it's easy to convert what we have from a synchronous to an asynchronous request handler. Let's say we receive a GET request with the data in the querystring and need to provide support for JSONP:

```
var http = require("http"),
  querystring = require("querystring");

http.createServer(function(req, res) {
  var qs = querystring.parse(req.url.split("?")[1]),
    username = qs.firstName + " " + qs.lastName,
    json;

  if (qs.callback) {
    // if we have a callback function name, do JSONP
    json = qs.callback + "({username:'" + username + "'});";
  } else {
    // otherwise, just return JSON
    json = JSON.stringify({"username":username});
  }

  res.writeHead(200, {
    // change MIME type to JSON
    "Content-Type": "application/json",
    "Content-Length": json.length
  });
  res.end(json);
}).listen(8000);
```

Even if we were using some sort of abstraction on top of Node itself, we'd probably just need to change the MIME type of our response to work with asynchronous requests and responses. There's also middleware that deals with this case specifically, and a wide variety of modules for adding real-time functionality. But the most basic asynchronous request handling doesn't require much more code than we'd need to write if we were using middleware.

Real-Time Communication

When Ajax showed up, it ushered in a new way of thinking about web requests. It was no longer necessary to request entire pages—we could communicate with the server in pure data. The server still had to wait for requests from the client, however. A client could poll the server for updates, but there was no way for the server to push new information to the client. The WebSockets API is part of the large collection of new standards being developed under the name HTML5, and allows the server and the client to open a bidirectional connection so that data can be pushed back and forth whenever necessary.

WebSockets and the various fallbacks used to mimic them aren't a technology specific to Node, but they make a very tidy fit. WebSockets *are* controlled with JavaScript, and the way they work looks an awful lot like the type of event handling we're used to in JavaScript. As we move toward applications that anticipate users' needs, perform non-essential operations in the background and report status, or just offer users a window into what's happening on the server as it happens, WebSockets become increasingly necessary. One or two real-time features might be easy enough to handle with long polling or some other method, but an entire real-time application warrants the use of the only truly appropriate technology.

One of the more popular and mature Node modules is Socket.IO, which wraps up WebSockets and a selection of fallbacks and exposes the functionality via an API that matches Node's EventEmitter. Socket.IO simplifies asynchronous requests dramatically, replacing listeners for requests with subscribers to events. The API is the same on the client or the server, so it feels more like the events are truly shared, even though they have to be treated very differently on either side.

To handle the asynchronous request above using WebSockets instead of a traditional XHR, we'd first need to set up our client-side code. We haven't really discussed the client's JavaScript because in most cases it should look exactly as it would for any other server. There are a number of Node modules, however, that have client-side components, so it's not unusual to require a module on the server and import the same thing or its complement on the client. Getting Socket.IO set up is pretty easy on both sides. The client-side code looks like this:

```
<input type="text" id="txtFirstName" placeholder="First name" />
<input type="text" id="txtLastName" placeholder="Last name" />
<input type="button" id="btnGetName" value="Save" />
<script src="http://localhost:1337/socket.io/socket.io.js"></script>
<script>
var socket = io.connect("http://localhost:1337"),
  fName = document.getElementById("txtFirstName"),
  lName = document.getElementById("txtLastName"),
  btn = document.getElementById("btnGetName");

// handle button click
btn.addEventListener("click", function() {
  // publish setName event with data
  socket.emit("setName", {firstName: fName.value, lastName: lName.value});
  return false;
});

// listen for nameSet event
socket.on("nameSet", function(data) {
  alert("Username set: " + data.userName);
});
</script>
```

Socket.IO is installed like any other published package, with the command npm install socket.io. When you install it, you may notice that it doesn't build the socket.io directory referenced in the src of our client-side JavaScript. However, you may also notice that we're getting that script file from a different port on our server. That's the port our

Socket.IO server will listen on, which we'll set up when we initialize it on the back-end. It will then provide its own client-side script.

We've now got a way to submit information from our form fields and a handler for when the response comes back. If this seems considerably more trim and decoupled than a traditional XHR, it should. Although there's a lot of logic going on behind the scenes, Socket.IO offers single-line abstractions that match the on/emit publish and subscribe API used by EventEmitter. We have Connect code in here as well to serve our page, but otherwise the server side looks much like the client:

```
var connect = require("connect"),
  // create socket.io server on port 1337
  io = require("socket.io").listen(1337);

connect(connect.static(__dirname + "/public")).listen(8000);

// listen for connection from an individual client
io.sockets.on("connection", function(socket) {
  // listen for setName event
  socket.on("setName", function(data) {
    var userName = data.firstName + " " + data.lastName;
    // publish nameSet event with new username
    socket.emit("nameSet", {userName: userName});
  });
});
```

Socket.IO can listen on its own port, or the same one used by the HTTP server—here we've assigned it port 1337 (any available port will do) and let Connect continue to use 8000. The Socket.IO server listens for each connection and, within that listener's callback, maintains a reference to the socket between the server and the individual client that connected. With that set up, we can publish and subscribe to events the same way we did on the client. As with the client, this code can be very simple. If you're already using Socket.IO for a few real-time features in an application, it can be tempting to do all your asynchronous requests with Socket.IO, since it makes communication so easy.

CHAPTER 4

Server-Side Templates

Most front-end developers have needed to work with server-side templates at some point. They may not have been called that—there was a time when these templates were simply called "PHP pages", "JSPs", or similar, before the push to apply separation of concerns on the web. These days it's more common to see pages and views rendered by any back-end framework trimmed of as much business logic as possible.

Node is no different. Just as those other application frameworks need a way to separate the HTML produced from the data that populates it, so does ours. We want to be able to create a set of views loosely coupled to our application logic and have the application decide when to render them, and with what data.

Creating a Dynamic Page

Unlike other server frameworks, choosing Node does not implicitly choose the templating engine you'll use for creating pages. There existed several templating engines for JavaScript when Node was created, and that number has only grown since. Thanks to Node, we now have a large number of server-side-only engines as well. Almost every JavaScript library of sufficient size offers a template engine, Underscore probably being the smallest, and there are many standalone options. Node frameworks also tend to have a default. Express uses Jade out of the box, for instance. It doesn't really matter which you choose, as long as it meets your needs and is comfortable for you.

Some things you might look at when selecting a templating engine are:

Does it require any language besides JavaScript?
    If so, you won't be able to use it on the client.

Does it require the existence of a DOM?
    If so, you'll need to fake a DOM in Node to use it on the server—this can be done, but it adds another step, of course.

Does it allow templates to be compiled once and cached, before they're first rendered?
> This may be a concern if you want to do all your template parsing up front, or if you'll render the same template many times.

Are there any restrictions on where or how templates are read into the template engine functions?
> You may need to have templates come from a `script` element in the DOM, a module in Node, or from a string literal. Wherever your templates will be stored, you want a template engine that doesn't expect them to be elsewhere.

How much logic is allowed in the template?
> Some template engines aim to be logic-less, with a subset going as far as only allowing insertion of strings. Others will allow you to write blocks of JavaScript as long as you like within the template. Logic-less templates are often managed by an additional layer that prepares data for rendering. This aspect of the template engine can affect your architecture, so it's worth doing some research.

To keep things simple, we'll use Mustache templates for these examples. If you've never used a JavaScript template engine, Mustache is a good place to start because it's right in the middle of the logic/no-logic spectrum, offering a subset of functions but not access to the whole of JavaScript. Additionally, the same syntax is used in lots of other template engines, which is a bonus in case your site eventually requires something more powerful or more minimal.

We already set up our application to accept values from a form collecting our user's first and last name, but we never discussed the form itself. Moreover, we haven't done a thing to help our user out should they want to change their submitted name. Our first server-side template will be an edit page for our user's (somewhat limited) information:

```
<!doctype html>
<html>
  <head>
    <meta charset="utf-8">
    <title>Edit your user information</title>
  </head>
  <body>
    <h1>Edit your user information</h1>
    <form action="/" method="POST">
      <label>First name:
        <input type="text" name="firstName" value="{{firstName}}" />
      </label>
      <label>Last name:
        <input type="text" name="lastName" value="{{lastName}}" />
      </label>
      <input type="submit" value="Save" />
    </form>
  </body>
</html>
```

The double curly braces around `firstName` and `lastName` are the delimiters that tell Mustache where to substitute in the data we'll pass it when it's time to render the page.

We're using the same property names for the existing values as we use for the name of the input elements to make things easy to keep track of, but the name, ID, and CSS class in the HTML are irrelevant to Mustache (which is one way it differs from some other template engines). To use our template, we need to install Mustache with npm, then modify our existing code to render the template instead of building the response HTML out of concatenated strings:

```
var connect = require("connect"),
  fs = require("fs"),
  mustache = require("mustache");

connect(
  connect.bodyParser(),
  function(req, res) {
    var userName = {
        firstName: req.body.firstName,
        lastName: req.body.lastName
      },
      // create and open the stream
      tmplFile = fs.createReadStream(
        __dirname + "/public/edit.html",
        {encoding: "utf8"}
      ),
      template = "",
      html;

    tmplFile.on("data", function(data) {
      template += data;
    });
    tmplFile.on("end", function() {

      // render the template with the userName object as data
      html = mustache.to_html(template, userName);

      res.end(html);

    });
  }
).listen(8000);
```

Assuming we stored our template as edit.html in the public directory, this code will stream the contents into a variable in our application and, once the template is fully loaded, pass it the submitted first and last name to render as HTML. Then we send the HTML back like we normally would.

We've switched from fs.readFile() to reading the template content from a stream above, which would normally make things more efficient, except that we don't need to load these templates over and over again or wait for them to be requested to know we'll need them. Going forward, we'll treat our templates as dependencies, and load them accordingly. It's good to note that there's more than one way to read a file, though.

Partial Templates

There will be certain pieces of the pages in our site that are repeated. Things like headers, footers, and certain application-specific widgets will appear on multiple pages, or every page. We could copy the markup for those pieces into the page's template, but it will be easier to manage a single shared template for each of these common elements. Copying and pasting a reference to a child template is more maintainable than copying and pasting the markup itself. If we don't want to have to repeat the code that imports our CSS and client-side JavaScript, we can templatize a default version of the pages in our site, storing all that information there, in addition to site-wide headers and footers. We can leave a space for the content of each page and reuse the rest. Let's create a file with this boilerplate markup called `parent.html`:

```
<!doctype html>
<html>
  <head>
    <meta charset="utf-8">
    <title>{{pageTitle}}</title>
    <link rel="stylesheet" src="css/style.css" />
    {{>stylesheets}}
  </head>
  <body>
    {{>content}}
    <footer>&copy; 2011 Node for Front-End Developers</footer>
  </body>
  {{>scripts}}
</html>
```

Every template engine handles nested templates differently. While Mustache uses the `{{>...}}` syntax you see above, templating engines that are otherwise very similar to Mustache may use something different. Try not to get too caught up in the particular syntax of this engine, just know that the greater-than sign here indicates a child template, and we'll use that to do composition.

To allow this parent template to load individual child templates and create full pages, we'll have to add some robustness into our application code. Instead of loading and rendering templates inline, we'll load another third-party module to manage loading, and move rendering to its own function.

The `requirejs` module works like the client-side Require.js utility, providing a slightly different approach to dependency management than Node's. The difference we're taking advantage of below is the `text.js` extension. We'll need to download this from the Require.js site and save it in our Node application's root directory. This will allow Require to load and manage text files, guaranteeing that they're loaded efficiently and available when they're needed. Adding the prefix `text!` to the path of the dependency (our template, in this case) tells Require to load the file as text instead of trying to evaluate it:

```
var connect = require("connect"),
  fs = require("fs"),
  mustache = require("mustache"),
  requirejs = require("requirejs"),
  parentTmpl;

// configure requirejs to fall back to Node's require if a module is not found
requirejs.config({ nodeRequire: require });

connect(
  connect.static(__dirname + "/public"),
  connect.router(function(app) {
    app.get("/show/:tmpl/:firstName/:lastName", function(req, res) {
      var userName = {
          firstName: req.params.firstName,
          lastName: req.params.lastName
        };
      // once the parent template is loaded, render the page
      requirejs(["text!public/parent.html"], function(_parentTmpl) {
        parentTmpl = _parentTmpl;
        render(res, req.params.tmpl + ".html", userName);
      });
    });
  })
).listen(8000);

function render(res, filename, data, style, script, callback) {
  // load the template and return control to another function or send the response
  requirejs(["text!public/" + filename], function(tmpl) {
    if (callback) {
      callback(res, tmpl, data, style, script);
    } else {
      // render parent template with page template as a child
      var html = mustache.to_html(
        parentTmpl,
        {content: data},
        {content: tmpl, stylesheets: style || "", scripts: script || ""}
      );
      res.end(html);
    }
  });
}
```

While we could make our system for rendering templates within a wrapper far more robust, this smaller amount of code will let us do quite a bit (within certain constraints). In addition to the content for each page, our parent template and its rendering function will accept additional CSS or JavaScript imports as string literals. We can allow the render function to send back the rendered HTML without modification, or we can override that behavior by passing in an additional callback to call once the child template loads.

Now that we have files being loaded and requests being made in order, you can begin to see the issues with nesting callbacks that frighten some people who are new to Node.

We've abstracted out some functionality, but there are still anonymous functions and nested logic. If you're used to DOM scripting, this probably isn't as scary, but you've probably also recognized it as something that needs to be managed. Although the code above is all in a single file for clarity, in a real application we'd put all of our template rendering code into its own module and move the logic into named functions private to that module.

Parsing Other File Types

If we wanted to dynamically generate CSS (maybe for use in a theme builder of some sort) or JavaScript (perhaps cherry-picking pieces of a more comprehensive JS library), all we have to do is change the file type we're reading in. Because we read in the files as strings, it makes no difference if they're something Node could technically try to execute. Here again, Node's lack of out-of-the-box handling for common file types works to our advantage. Any file can be an application, a library, a template, or a static resource—it's entirely up to us and how we treat it.

Let's say that we do indeed have a site offering some kind of customizable client-side widget library. For example, assume we have a customizable CSS file using Mustache to populate user-defined values:

```
h1 { color: #{{main}}; }
h2 { color: #{{secondary}}; }
input { border-style: {{border}}; border-radius: {{corners}}px; }
```

To provide our end users with CSS and JavaScript matching their site's needs, we only really need to change our routing. We'll assume the values we're receiving are coming from a form post, and that the rest of our application file remains the same:

```
connect(
  connect.static(__dirname + "/public"),
  connect.bodyParser(),
  connect.router(function(app) {
    app.post("/theme", function(req, res) {
      var theme = {
        main: req.body.mainColor,
        secondary: req.body.secondaryColor,
        border: req.body.borderStyle,
        corners: req.body.borderRadius
      };
      // load and render the CSS template
      requirejs(["text!public/css/theme.css"], function(tmpl) {
        var css = mustache.to_html(tmpl, theme);
        res.writeHead(200, {
          "Content-Type": "text/css",
          "Content-Length": css.length
        });
        res.end(css);
      });
    };
```

```
app.post("/builder", function(req, res) {
    var options = {
      shim: req.body.html5shim,
      flash: req.body.useFlash,
      sockets: req.body.useWebSockets,
      jsonp: req.body.useJsonp
    };
    // load and render the JS template
    requirejs(["text!public/js/builder.js"], function(tmpl) {
      var js = mustache.to_html(tmpl, options);
      res.writeHead(200, {
        "Content-Type": "application/javascript",
        "Content-Length": js.length
      });
      res.end(js);
    });
  };
})
).listen(8000);
```

Since we don't want our CSS or JavaScript composed into our parent template, we can skip the render function and recreate its functionality for both MIME types we'll want to return. You can probably see how the logic to render and return a response could be abstracted out into a function of its own, but since our example application only handles these two scenarios, the less efficient code above will get the job done.

Creating Files on the Fly

An in-depth exploration of any of the necessary modules is out of scope for this guide, but there are numerous libraries to help you generate other types of files from within Node. While these aren't templates in the same sense as the templates we've looked at so far, they can map directly to a filename in a URL and be built and served in a way that's invisible to the user, just like templates. For instance, you might have cause to dynamically generate image files to do resizing or add watermarks. Modules to do that will have their own APIs, and can be loaded and used like any template engine or other module. To keep your application code clean, you'd probably choose to keep the code you write to work with those APIs in a separate file, the same way an external template stores information specific to rendering HTML or other text-based file types.

CHAPTER 5

Data Sources and Flow Control

Up until now, the client has been able to get whatever it needs more or less immediately. We wait for our end user to initiate a request, but that user never waits for the application. Of course, that isn't how real web applications work. Dynamic data requires some sort of data storage, and working with a data store takes time. When our user initiates a request to the server, the application on the server may, in turn, need to initiate its own request to a database, and will not be able to respond to the user until a response comes from the data source. While connecting to a database is a necessary function in itself, it's also a good place to discuss server-side flow control.

Connecting to a Database

If you have some experience dealing with databases in other server frameworks, thinking about the way it's done in Node can be a bit tricky. Firstly, Node has no default way of connecting to a database. Depending on your experience, you may have worked with ODBC or JDBC (Open Database Connectivity and Java Database Connectivity, respectively). No analogue to those things exists in Node. A database will provide its own API and you will connect directly to that. The only thing shared between Node itself and the database will be the EventEmitter vocabulary, if that.

The second trick is that there are a lot of different ways people choose to store data in Node. If you're used to .NET on the back-end, you probably expect to use SQL Server. If you've worked with the traditional LAMP stack, MySQL is the natural database choice for your projects. This is slightly more complicated in Node because you can use anything you like. There are a number of data stores that use key-value patterns similar to JSON, but nothing precludes use of a traditional relational database like MySQL. When choosing a database for Node, it's most important that you know what kind of data you'd like to store and your priorities regarding how it's stored. For instance, a data store that's very fast but won't alert you if it fails to store a piece of data could be useful for caching trivial session information, but not for saving users' privacy settings. If necessary, you can combine solutions so that you're using the best tool for each individual job.

For this example we'll choose one of the simplest, Redis. Redis is used for caching by a number of real-world Node applications. It's not feature-rich, but it's very fast and the object structure will be immediately familiar to anyone used to JSON. Getting it set up is easy—much easier than setting up a database would be in many traditional server-side frameworks. It's still a two-step installation process, because we need to install the Redis server itself (instructions are available on the Redis site at `redis.io`) and also the `redis` Node interface from npm, but after that it's smooth sailing. Just as we create a client listening for requests from the front-end, we'll create a client for interacting with Redis. We can then get and set simple (or not so simple) key/value pairs. Here we'll assume that each `lastName` is stored under the `firstName` it belongs to:

```
var http = require("http"),
  querystring = require("querystring"),
  redis = require("redis"),
  // create a redis client on redis' default port
  db = redis.createClient(6379, "127.0.0.1");

http.createServer(function(req, res) {
  var qs = querystring.parse(req.url.split("?")[1]),
    firstName = qs.firstName;

  // get the last name for the submitted first name and render
  db.get(firstName, function(err, lastName) {
    var userName = firstName + " " + lastName,
      html = "<!doctype html>" +
        "<html><head><title>Hello " + userName + "</title></head>" +
        "<body><h1>Hello, " + userName + "!</h1></body></html>";

    res.end(html);
  });
}).listen(8000);
```

Since we haven't set any data for the key we're searching for, the `lastName` variable will be null. However, you can add a line before `http.createServer()` to create a key and value in your data store so you see real results:

```
db.set("Jaime", "Developer", function(){});
```

We think of requests to and responses from a data store as being synchronous in traditional back-end programming, but in Node they're asynchronous, like almost everything else. That means the results of our "query" will come back when they come back, and we need to provide a handler for that event, rather than assuming they'll be available to subsequent code. In theory it might be fast enough to return a single value, but if we started returning significant amounts of data, it would become clear why we process the results from within a callback. We're not working with a lot of data in these examples, but if we change our simple key/value to a hash, hopefully it becomes apparent how we could:

```
var http = require("http"),
  querystring = require("querystring"),
  redis = require("redis"),
  db = redis.createClient(6379, "127.0.0.1");

http.createServer(function(req, res) {
  var qs = querystring.parse(req.url.split("?")[1]),
    firstName = qs.firstName,
    userName,
    page;

  // get the value of the firstName key from within the users hash
  db.hget("users", firstName, function(err, value) {
    if (err) {
      throw err;
    }
    userName = firstName + " " + value;
    html = "<!doctype html>" +
      "<html><head><title>Hello " + userName + "</title></head>" +
      "<body><h1>Hello, " + userName + "!</h1></body></html>";

    res.end(html);
  });
}).listen(8000);
```

As before, you'll have to add some data to see the page return anything besides null. This time, use:

```
db.hset("users", "Jaime", "Developer", function(){});
```

The hset function treats users as a hash, and sets the value for a key within it.

Hardcoding data isn't very scalable and runs counter to the purpose of having a data store in the first place. Long term, our data has to come from somewhere, so let's return to our hypothetical user info edit page and make the data submitted there persistent. In this particular data store, creating a "record" is as easy as creating a property on an object in JavaScript. We provide the key and the value and that pair is stored. In this case there's no reason to wait for the response to return, strictly speaking, but we can optionally wait until we receive a response to provide the HTML to the client, mimicking what a traditional server would do:

```
var connect = require("connect"),
  redis = require("redis"),
  db = redis.createClient(6379, "127.0.0.1");

connect(
  connect.static(__dirname + "/public"),
  connect.bodyParser(),
  function(req, res) {
    var firstName = req.body.firstName,
      lastName = req.body.lastName,
      userName = firstName + " " + lastName;
```

```
// store the submitted lastName using the firstName as a key
db.hset("users", firstName, lastName, function(err, response) {
  var html = "<!doctype html>" +
    "<html><head><title>Hello " + userName + "</title></head>" +
    "<body><h1>Hello, " + userName + "!</h1></body></html>";

  res.end(html);
});
}
).listen(8000);
```

This is the most simplistic example of using Redis possible—it can store hashes and lists and approximate complex data types that would be useful in real-world applications, as well as incrementing IDs to provide unique keys for data. Other non-relational solutions do those things as well, and of course relational databases do them very competently. Any one, or a combination, of these is a valid architectural choice in Node, so we won't go any further into the specifics.

Storing Data in Files

Though you probably wouldn't choose to store data in a text file over a database, there might be times when you want to write to and read from something highly portable— for example, if you were managing values in a config file. Writing to a file can't give us the control over individual properties a data store can, of course, and it's very slow, but there are still applications where a text file makes sense. Like writing to a database, writing to a file is done asynchronously, so if we want verification that it was done we'll need to take any dependent actions from within a callback:

```
var connect = require("connect"),
  fs = require("fs");

connect(
  connect.static(__dirname + "/public"),
  connect.bodyParser(),
  function(req, res) {
    var firstName = req.body.firstName,
      lastName = req.body.lastName,
      userName = firstName + " " + lastName,
      stream;

    if (firstName || lastName) {
      // create a stream, and create the file if it doesn't exist
      stream = fs.createWriteStream("user_name.txt");
    } else {
      return;
    }

    stream.on("open", function() {
      // write to and close the stream at the same time
      stream.end((firstName + "," + lastName + "\n"), "utf-8");
      var html = "<!doctype html>" +
```

```
            "<html><head><title>Hello " + userName + "</title></head>" +
            "<body><h1>Hello, " + userName + "!</h1></body></html>";

        res.end(html);
    });
  }
).listen(8000);
```

Setting the data is easy, but it's also fragile. We have to check that we've actually received data to avoid overwriting good data with bad, and if we had multiple users trying to update a file, this would be a huge mess. To create a robust, real-world implementation, we'd have to establish a system of locking the file while writing to it. The more advanced extensions to the native fs module provide this, and other useful features.

Getting the data back out of the text file is less fraught with danger and works just like pulling in any of our static files or templates. To get the data contained, we need to split the text apart by whatever we used to concatenate it. Our example is just a comma-separated value file, so we split on the comma. If we had more than one "row" of data, we could then further split the individual rows out into a matrix representing them:

```
var stream = fs.createReadStream("user_name.txt"),
  vals = "",
  users;

stream.on("data", function(data) {
  vals += data;
});
stream.on("end", function() {
  users = vals.split("\n").split(",");
});
```

Callbacks and Messaging

Few things we've done up to this point have *not* been done within a callback. Granted, these are extremely simple examples meant to demonstrate atomic concepts, not complete applications, but that doesn't mean things would necessarily be different in a full application. On the client-side, it's possible to get fairly long JavaScript functions doing initializations or handling a complex piece of front-end processing. That same thing is possible on the server, but it's something to watch out for. Node excels at responding to events, but tasks requiring large amounts of back-end processing are places where it's unlikely to shine.

Of course, the client-side is all about events or, more specifically, their handlers. Shocking numbers of people got their start with JavaScript writing (or copying and pasting) an image rollover. In DOM scripting, we tend to respond to events but not generate them—but if you've built large single-page applications you've probably done plenty of both. You could say that events are the way Node thinks. Rather than write long blocks of monolithic code or nest callbacks several levels deep, we can create nicer code by emulating the client-side and treating everything we possibly can as an event handler.

Implementations of messaging range from trivial to complex, both on their own and as part of larger frameworks. However, they all do essentially the same thing, assigning subscribers to event names and then, once an event is triggered, invoking those subscribers. Because EventEmitter provides basic functions for publishing and subscribing already, it's easy to create a wrapper that exposes EventEmitter's main functions in a generic way:

```
var util = require("util"),
  events = require("events");

var PubSub = function() {
  events.EventEmitter.call(this);
  return this;
};

// add the properties of EventEmitter to PubSub
util.inherits(PubSub, events.EventEmitter);

// expose instances of PubSub when the module is consumed
exports.PubSub = PubSub;
```

Modules don't look much different than an external script file you might use on the client-side, but there's one difference you definitely must be aware of: the exports keyword. exports allows you to define the parts of your module that will be exposed to code that imports the module. If you don't assign a value or properties to exports, your module's functionality won't be available in other files. This is a crucial difference between Node and the client-side, where you're often more concerned with keeping things out of the global scope than with how to expose them.

This is slightly silly, but it gets the silliness out of our application and makes it reusable. We can save this file in our lib directory as pubsub.js and then use it from our code like so:

```
var p = require("./lib/pubsub.js").PubSub,
  pubsub = new p();

pubsub.on("sayHello", function() {
  console.log("Hello, developer.");
});

pubsub.emit("sayHello");
```

More practically, we could move subscribers into external files and publish events from the main workflow of our application or individual routes, making our code tidier and more reusable. As long as we retain access to the same pubsub object, we can organize our code however we want and are able to control the path of execution by publishing individual events. This is very useful if, for instance, you need to load a template, get some data from a data store, and update an application log when a certain event takes place. Those separate operations can remain separate. If they aren't separate, one event's handler can trigger the next and execution can be chained. There are more sophisticated ways of handling flow control, of course, but at their core they're all just passing messages.

CHAPTER 6

Model-View-Controller
and Sharing Code

One of the great things about Node is that it can take advantage of the lessons of all the web development frameworks that came before it. Modern architectures tend to follow the Model-View-Controller pattern to decouple the pieces of an application and make working with the code easier. To affect meaningful separation of concerns, however, the views created in MVC on the web must be completely dumb, without the ability to manage even their presentational logic. The alternative is the duplication of some code between the server and client, which can become difficult to maintain. Since Node's client-side code can also run on the server (and vice versa) we can take interesting steps toward improving architectures and reusing code.

Implementing the MVC Pattern

How MVC is used on the client, if at all, varies depending on the needs of the application, but the trend is inarguably toward architectures that borrow from the pattern. This makes sense, as we often have the need to maintain a snapshot of our data while moving through an application that doesn't interact with the server frequently, yet we still need the same DOM interactions the front-end has always needed. And of course we need the code that defines the path through the application and the code to render new pages or metaphors for pages. As soon as we decide to do any of that work on the server, it's probably not surprising that we need the same things, and we've already implemented bits and pieces.

One of the most popular Node modules for organizing applications is Express. Express builds on Connect, which we've looked at. The syntax for Express looks a lot like Connect, but Express provides a cohesive framework, instead of an a la carte toolkit. Express isn't a strict implementation of MVC, but it builds in separation of concerns, so we can make small changes to get a more literal interpretation of the pattern.

A nice feature of Express if you're getting started with it or with Node is that it can set up a skeletal application for you. After installing Express with npm, you can run this script from the root of your site and have it set up a directory structure and a few example files for you:

```
./node_modules/express/bin/express
```

Once Express sets up its directory structure, you'll see that the only leg of MVC explicitly provided out of the box is the view layer. We don't have a single, application-wide controller, but the routing functionality allows us to create small, decoupled controllers that map data models to view rendering code. This leaves us to create the models themselves—presumably as separate modules, so any business logic or data storage can be handled outside of the flow of the interactions with the client.

Returning to the simplistic picture of a user who's just a first name and a last name, we can set up a model, view, and controller (that is, a set of routes) for managing that concept pretty easily using what we already know about Express, thanks to its use of Connect and the other concepts we've looked at. First, though, let's create a module called user.js to represent a user. You can save it in lib, or in a models directory if you want to reserve lib for utility code unrelated to any specific model. To make it more realistic, we'll add an ID in case multiple users share the same first name:

```
var redis = require("redis"),
  db = redis.createClient(6379, "127.0.0.1"),
  userFunctions = {
    // create a new user
    add: function(firstName, lastName, cb) {
      // get the current count of users plus one for use as an ID
      db.incr("userCount", function(err, id) {
        if (err)
          throw err;
        db.hmset("users:" + id, {"firstName": firstName, "lastName": lastName},
          function(err) {
            if (!err && cb)
              cb(id);
          });
      });
    },
    // edit an existing user
    change: function(id, firstName, lastName, cb) {
      db.hmset("users:" + id, {"firstName": firstName, "lastName": lastName},
        function(err) {
          if (!err && cb)
            cb(id);
        });
    },
    // retrieve a user object
    getUser: function(id, cb) {
      db.hgetall("users:" + id,
        function(err, user) {
          if (!err)
            cb(user);
```

```
      });
    },
    // retrieve a user object and concatenate the name
    getUserName: function(id, cb) {
      db.hgetall("users:" + id,
        function(err, user) {
          if (!err)
            cb(user.firstName + " " + user.lastName);
        });
    },
    // delete a user
    deleteUser: function(id, cb) {
      db.del("users:" + id,
        function(err) {
          if (!err && cb)
            cb();
        });
    }
  };

  // expose our object as the userFunctions property of this module
  exports.userFunctions = userFunctions;
```

Now we have a model that takes care of persisting and retrieving our data, and provides some nominal business logic by concatenating the user name in case we want to immediately use it in a view. It's worth noting that we could use our pubsub utility here to avoid some of these nested callbacks. No matter how we manage flow control, once we separate out the logic for interacting with the data store, any code that calls these functions will need to use some sort of callback if it wants a response, whether it's a traditional callback or a subscriber to a published event.

We already have a views directory, so let's add a template to display and edit the user. Express uses the Jade template engine by default, but we can switch it to use any Express-compatible engine we like. Moreover, if our preferred template engine hasn't been packaged up to work with Express, it's trivial to add the functionality ourselves. Since Jade is the default, we'll use it for this example, but you should choose the template engine that best fits your application's needs. Jade templates use a markdown style that looks much different from Mustache, and from HTML:

```
- if (username.length)
    h1= username
- else
    form(action="/save",method="POST")
        input#hdnId(name="hdnId", type="hidden", value=user.id)
        input#txtFirstName(name="txtFirstName", type="text", value=user.firstName)
        input#txtLastName(name="txtLastName", type="text", value=user.lastName)
        input#btnGetName(type="button", value="Save")
        input#btnDelete(type="button", value="Delete User")
    script
        document.getElementById("btnGetName").addEventListener("click", function() {
            this.parentNode.submit();
        });
```

```
        document.getElementById("btnDelete").addEventListener("click", function() {
            var form = this.parentNode;
            this.parentNode.action = "/delete/" +
document.getElementById("hdnId").value;
            this.parentNode.submit();
        });
```

If you decide to use Jade, note that whitespace in Jade is significant, so things are only nested logically if they're nested physically. You may also note that there is no **doctype** or **head** in the template above. No matter which template engine it uses, Express expects a layout file containing common page elements—we did the same thing with our parent template earlier. If we save this file as **user.jade** in our **views** directory, we've got our view layer wrapped up. The last thing we need to do is to create a controller.

There are any number of ways to break our application up in terms of where we define the routes that will act as our controllers, but for now let's just add a **users.js** file to our **routes** directory and keep the callbacks for our request listeners there:

```
var user = require("../models/user").userFunctions,
  // empty user definition to prevent Jade choking on undefined values
  emptyUser = {
    id: "",
    firstName: "",
    lastName: ""
  };

// display user data
exports.show = function show(req, res) {
  user.getUserName(req.params.id, function(username) {
    res.render("user", {username: username, user: emptyUser});
  });
}

// show add new user form
exports.add = function add(req, res) {
  res.render("user", {username: "", user: emptyUser});
}

// show edit user form
exports.edit = function edit(req, res) {
  var id = req.params.id;
  user.getUser(id, function(user) {
    user.id = id;
    res.render("user", {username: "", user: user});
  });
}

// save changes to a new or existing user
exports.save = function save(req, res) {
  var id = req.body.hdnId,
    firstName = req.body.txtFirstName,
    lastName = req.body.txtLastName,
    callback = function(id) {
      res.render("user", {username: "", user:
```

```
        {id: id,
          firstName: firstName,
          lastName: lastName}
      });
    };
  if (id) {
    // edit user information if ID is present
    user.change(id, firstName, lastName, callback);
  } else {
    // otherwise add new user
    user.add(firstName, lastName, callback);
  }
}

// delete a user
exports.del = function del(req, res) {
  user.deleteUser(req.params.id, function() {
    res.render("index");
  });
}
```

These controllers for the user object will route the application to the correct view, depending on the request and parameters received, or initiate tasks on the user model. In Express, we access parameters sent with the request the same way we would with Connect alone, so the syntax should look familiar. For example, our **save** function gets posted values from **req.body** because Express uses the same **bodyParser** as Connect to attach the values to the request.

The last thing we need to do is wire this controller logic up to our main application file:

```
var express = require("express"),
  app = express.createServer(),
  user = require("./routes/users");

// boilerplate configuration added by Express
app.configure(function(){
  app.set('views', __dirname + '/views');
  app.set('view engine', 'jade');
  app.use(express.bodyParser());
  app.use(express.methodOverride());
  app.use(app.router);
  app.use(express.static(__dirname + '/public'));
});

app.get("/profile/:id", user.show);
app.get("/edit", user.add);
app.get("/edit/:id", user.edit);
app.post("/save", user.save);
app.post("/delete/:id", user.del);
app.get("/", function(req, res) {
  res.render("index",{title:"Hello world"});
});

app.listen(8000);
```

As MVC implementations go, this is far from fancy, but it does accomplish MVC's main goal of decoupling pieces of the application. We could introduce an entirely different model for our users and the main application code wouldn't need to change at all. We could switch from Redis to CouchDB for our data storage without affecting anything outside of the `models` directory. This is a little closer to what a real-world Node application might look like. Relying on the tools that Express or another application framework provides and a selection of Node modules to provide additional functionality, you should be able to scale this sort of simple structure to meet your needs.

Out-of-the-Box MVC

Because of the popularity of client-side MVC, you may have an existing client-side architecture you want to port over to Node. That's especially true if you have concerns about JavaScript not being present or not being current on the client.

One of the more popular MVC frameworks is Backbone.js. Backbone is available as a CommonJS module in npm and tries to be non-DOM-centric, so it makes a nice fit for Node. If you're using Backbone, you've probably realized that your models, collections, and templates could be reused on the server with minimal effort. You may also have noticed a caveat that would never be an issue on the client-side: there's no shared global namespace from which all the components of a Backbone application can be accessed. If you've separated your client-side code out into nicely organized files, that actually creates a disadvantage in Node. Objects not sharing the scope of the same module will have to be explicitly passed around. One possible way to deal with this is to create a single module that requires all your other Backbone files, reassembling the namespace you would have created client-side and exposing the entire client-side app in a single object:

```
var main = require("../public/js/lib/main"),
    user = require("../public/js/lib/modules/user");

var BackboneApp = {
  application: main,
  modules: {
    user: user
  }
};

exports.app = BackboneApp;
```

In the next section we'll deal with how to build modules that work on either the client or server, but note for the moment that references to any object in any other module will need to be passed to child modules on initialization, or as needed. It may be worth combining models, views, and controllers into one module where possible, to reduce the number of objects you have to pass around.

You could import your models, collections, and templates and leave it at that, but you can also extend your code to do server-only operations. For example, you'll probably want to persist the data in your models to a data store when they change. Because Backbone provides custom events your code can subscribe to, you should be able to put listeners in a separate file available only to Node and handle server-only operations without needing to check the context in which the model code is running.

After we import a Backbone application's models and templates, we'll begin to see diminishing returns if we continue trying to reuse things. We can use the routes defined in the application, but we may not use them in the same way. The server will need its own views, with render functions, to allow callbacks for many routes to work correctly. Consuming routes, of course, will be completely different. Instead of managing the client-side history of an application, we'll be manually mapping Backbone's routes to patterns in whatever our HTTP server uses for routing.

There are a number of modules available to help you work with Backbone applications in Node, and it's definitely the client-side framework with the most mature support for use with Node. There are numerous modules, for instance, to help you store data and reuse Backbone data models. Depending on how much of an application needs to be shared, working with one or more of those tools may be very useful. Node moves fast, so if you use another client-side MVC framework, it's definitely worth checking npm to see if someone has ported your framework of choice over for use with Node.

Sharing Modules Between the Client and Server

Files within your application's `public` directory can be served by your application, of course, by they can also be used by it. If there's a module providing some business logic you need for both the client and server, it's fragile to try and store it in two places—the better strategy is to reference it from a single location. If you're using Require.js or similar on the client-side this is very easy because you can import the module the same way in both places, but even if you're not, you can share code.

Because of the possibilities that reusing client-side code offers, there are numerous utilities to create an unrendered DOM in Node, enabling client-side code to run un-modified on the server. These things aren't likely to disappear—they can be necessary for scraping or spidering content, for example. Because `window` or `document` objects may be created on the server by these tools, in shared modules it's safer to test whether we're on the server-side than whether we're on the client. One way to do this is to look for the `process` object:

```
(function(ns) {
  ns.modul = function() {
    console.log("works!");
  };
  return ns;
}((typeof process !== "undefined" && process.title === "node")
    ? exports : myapp));
```

On the server, this will pass exports into our function to use as a parent object. On the client, we can hardcode the global namespace being used there. Our module will attach whatever it exposes to that object without having to worry about the context it's running in, and either make our code available globally (client-side) or allow it to be imported (server-side). Of course, utilities like Require.js for managing modules can be used on either the client or server, so if you're building a new application, creating shared code as CommonJS modules in the first place will make this all very easy.

Postscript

At this point, hopefully you feel comfortable writing a Node.js application. If you have existing client-side JavaScript skills, there's little preventing you from setting up Node locally and beginning to write code. However, this book is not a complete guide to Node; there are important steps to take next, once you've gotten used to writing applications.

Because of Node's age, there are only a few established hosting providers providing setup and management. In contrast to Apache, for example, the number of options is tiny. Nonetheless, there are already companies who will manage Node for you, requiring you to do nothing more than upload your application code. If you feel comfortable with a more hands-on approach, a virtual private server that allows you SSH access will enable you to set up Node to your liking and control things from the command line.

We've covered application development here, but it's important not to go into programming for Node thinking that this is all there is to it. Just like any other server, for a production implementation, the expertise of someone who understands servers and systems administration is needed, at least to get set up. If you have that skill set, you should find it reasonably simple to track down modules and tools for administrative tasks like keeping Node running, creating logs, concatenating and compressing client-side files, etc. If you don't, your best bet is to look for a managed installation or team up with a friend who can handle or teach you to handle the systems side.

But don't let that scare you off! Node is showing up in production all over the place, and the more that happens, the better the options will be for handling its administration, freeing up JavaScript developers to focus on what they're best at. There's an enthusiastic community of developers you can reach out to in IRC, GitHub, or on Node's mailing list to get support, as well as a massive library of open source modules you can build your application on. Now is a great time to start learning Node, and begin working toward deploying your first live Node application.

About the Author

Garann returned to front-end development three years ago after spending several years working on back-ends. She started the Austin All-Girl Hack Night and teaches women to code as an instructor for Girl Develop It Austin. When she's not writing JavaScript, she's often operating some sort of power tool as she remodels her 111-year-old house.

Get even more for your money.

Join the O'Reilly Community, and register the O'Reilly books you own. It's free, and you'll get:

- $4.99 ebook upgrade offer
- 40% upgrade offer on O'Reilly print books
- Membership discounts on books and events
- Free lifetime updates to ebooks and videos
- Multiple ebook formats, DRM FREE
- Participation in the O'Reilly community
- Newsletters
- Account management
- 100% Satisfaction Guarantee

Signing up is easy:

1. **Go to: oreilly.com/go/register**
2. **Create an O'Reilly login.**
3. **Provide your address.**
4. **Register your books.**

Note: English-language books only

To order books online:
oreilly.com/store

For questions about products or an order:
orders@oreilly.com

To sign up to get topic-specific email announcements and/or news about upcoming books, conferences, special offers, and new technologies:
elists@oreilly.com

For technical questions about book content:
booktech@oreilly.com

To submit new book proposals to our editors:
proposals@oreilly.com

O'Reilly books are available in multiple DRM-free ebook formats. For more information:
oreilly.com/ebooks

O'REILLY®

Spreading the knowledge of innovators   oreilly.com

The information you need, when and where you need it.

With Safari Books Online, you can:

Access the contents of thousands of technology and business books

- Quickly search over 7000 books and certification guides
- Download whole books or chapters in PDF format, at no extra cost, to print or read on the go
- Copy and paste code
- Save up to 35% on O'Reilly print books
- **New!** Access mobile-friendly books directly from cell phones and mobile devices

Stay up-to-date on emerging topics before the books are published

- Get on-demand access to evolving manuscripts.
- Interact directly with authors of upcoming books

Explore thousands of hours of video on technology and design topics

- Learn from expert video tutorials
- Watch and replay recorded conference sessions

Lightning Source UK Ltd.
Milton Keynes UK
UKHW031124160621
385610UK00004B/96